C000177750

PEAKY BLINDERS

A History from Beginning to End

Table of Contents

Introduction

By the end of the nineteenth century, Britain was a blend of two worlds: the world of royalty, privilege, and prosperity, and another very different world that involved poverty, hardship, and destitution. It is in the latter that the Peaky Blinders were formed. The real Peaky Blinders were an urban street gang based in Birmingham, England at the end of the nineteenth century. They operated in the region right up to World War I, and several gang members even served in the war.

Living conditions in most cities and towns in Britain at this time can only be described as atrocious. Populations in cities and towns were growing, but many cities couldn't expand fast enough to accommodate the rapid growth. Because there wasn't enough housing to go around, rents increased sharply, and the result was that many people lived together in small spaces. The overcrowding resulted in the horrible living conditions associated with this time, and the Industrial Revolution only magnified the social problems.

Needless to say, in such crowded, unsanitary, and downright miserable living conditions, crime rates soared, but despite that, the police remained poorly funded and trained. In Birmingham at this time, the streets were filled with gambling dens and juvenile delinquents. People who belonged to the higher classes put pressure on the police to crack down on the rampant criminal activities, and in response to this crackdown, groups of young men and boys banded together in what were called "slogging gangs" to fight back.

One such slogging gang comprised of the most violent men and boys was known as the Peaky Blinders. This gang was likely formed in the Small Heath section of Birmingham, and it would go on to rule this part of Birmingham for the next decade. Named for their elegant manner of dress, the Peaky Blinders would amass—through violence—control that they would maintain for years. Their story has endured through time, becoming the inspiration for the BBC television series *Peaky Blinders*, and so fierce was their reputation that Peaky Blinders became a slang term for any street gang.

Chapter One

Life in Victorian Britain

"Whether the queen caused the period, or the period creates the queen, she fitted her time perfectly."

—Florence Becker Lennon, on Queen Victoria

Britain's population in the 1800s was booming, and people began flocking to the cities to find work and a better life. Because there weren't enough dwellings available, the rents soared and people had to live together in crowded and unsanitary conditions. Additionally, homeowners took little care of their properties, resulting in horrible slums. Added to poorly maintained properties was contaminated drinking water. The cities dumped their waste into channels that ran into the main rivers which, in turn, became the main sources for disease. The situation was so bad that London authorities estimated there were at least seven dead bodies in the River Thames at any given time.

As cities were packed to the brim with people struggling to support themselves and their families, it's not surprising that the crime rate rose precipitously, and as that happened, the police turned to public punishment as a deterrent. People convicted of serious crimes were hanged publicly and often tortured too. The situation was just about as bad as can be imagined, and for the most vulnerable, particularly children, it was darker still.

Child labor was common in the 1800s, particularly since children could be forced to work for hours, they tired less easily than adults, and they could be made to work in conditions where adults could not go, or where adults refused to go. And, of course, children were paid very little for their efforts. Thus, children often worked in production factories, in coal mines, and perhaps most famously, as chimney sweeps. They were well-suited for the latter since they were small and could easily fit into small spaces. It was dangerous work, however, and children frequently got stuck or died as a result of breathing in soot all day.

Contrasting the bleakness of many cities and towns in Britain was the obscene wealth of the upper class, and while the working class suffered, observing the ghastly conditions became a hobby of the very wealthy. They called their new hobby "slumming," and it involved dressing like the common people to go out and observe the atrocious living conditions. Their hobby did help to bring attention to the problems of the slum, and the conditions were debated in Parliament as humanitarian groups lobbied against the awful conditions, particularly for the children.

Like most other towns in Britain at this time, the conditions in Birmingham were unsanitary. In the second half of the nineteenth century, conditions started to improve because sewers were dug, but only new houses were required to connect to them. Existing houses would wait decades to be connected. The Birmingham Water Company provided piped water to the town, but the citizens had to pay for that service, and since many couldn't afford it, they continued to rely on well water or water carriers. So bad were the conditions in this town that in just one year, 3,400 children died before reaching the age of one.

Despite the improvements made in the sanitation conditions, there were still epidemics of smallpox in 1871-1872, 1874, and 1883. There were also two epidemics of scarlet fever—one in 1878 and another in 1882-1883. There were several asylums and a new general hospital that opened late in the century. Still, despite the improvements, the gap between the wealthy and the poor made for some very desperate conditions.

Chapter Two

Birmingham, the Birthplace of the Peaky Blinders

"The blood is painting the streets again
With hammers and razor blades
Thieves and riots are our daily bread
The Peaky Blinders prevail."

—"Cheapside Sloggers" by Volbeat

By 1801, Birmingham, with a population of 73,670, was one of England's most important towns. The industry in this town was dominated by metalworking, but there were also jewelers, gunsmiths, railway carriage and bicycle makers, glassmakers, and cocoa and chocolate makers.

Birmingham was famously described as "the great toy-shop of Europe" by philosopher Edmund Burke. What was meant by toys at that time were small metal items that involved intricate craftsmanship. These would be things like key-locks, bracelets, buckles, and nails—almost anything that can be fashioned from metal. By 1865, a few factories had sprung up, but the most typical manufacturers—jewelry and gun manufacturers—were still small masters and out workers. By the end of the nineteenth century, however, the factory would be the typical form of production, and machine tools were replacing skilled artisans. This meant that traditional hardware production was in decline. In fact, the manufacture of traditional crafts of all kinds was being overtaken by the factories.

Crime was pervasive in this industrial setting, and the types of crime drew heavily on the skills of metal manufacturers. Additionally, Birmingham was the home of the Baskerville print, and because of the printing tradition and metal skills found there, it became the home of forgers, especially for paper money. During the Napoleonic Wars, Birmingham had the dubious title of the "fountainhead" of forged banknotes. One of the most famous leaders of a forging gang was William Booth, who was eventually caught in the act of printing notes in 1812. He was sentenced to death, but the hangman's noose broke on the first attempt to hang him, and the trap door refused to open on the second try. It had to be forced open before Booth was finally hanged. His grave later became a tourist attraction.

Rather than deterring the forger industry in Birmingham, Booth's death seemed only to spur it on. Soon, gangs of "coiners" emerged, passing off forged coins in intricate schemes organized by the coin forger and his passers—those who would pass off the forged coins as legitimate. As police surveillance on these coin gangs grew, the coining forgery slowly died out. Many of the men involved in these schemes, particularly those who were younger, began looking for adventure on the streets instead.

With the gathering of labor into workshops and factories, conflicts with owners followed, and that resulted in occasional strikes, but violence between trades was far more common than within trades. It was in this setting that slogging was born. The term slogging originated with prizefighters, but in Birmingham, it had a slightly different meaning. Slogging was defined by the *Birmingham Daily Gazette* in 1873 as "mercilessly stoning passersby," although sloggers often used a variety of other weapons, such as belt buckles and knives. Slogging became more common during this time, and interestingly, the patterns of leisure were an important factor in its growth, particularly the dinner hour and the habit of going out on Sunday afternoons. Slogging in gangs was far more common on Sundays, the day for shopping, rest, and recreation.

Usually, slogging gangs consisted of street kids and rough young men between the ages of 12 and 30 years. These gangs were not afraid of the police and, in fact, they frequently fought them. As this went on, the gangs became emboldened and began to attack members of the public in broad daylight as they walked in the streets. Over time, these gangs were organized into what could be described as a soft hierarchy, whereby there was general recognition of who ranked higher, but nothing formal had been established.

Birmingham had a long tradition of fighting—even women proudly took part in street fights—and the ethnic tensions between Irish Catholics and Protestants provided fuel for ongoing battles. But, by far, the most contentious and hostile gangs were those that formed around trades. This was true despite the fact that slogging gangs were not composed exclusively of members of one trade. Many gangs also included unemployed people or those simply described as laborers. Often, the territories of various slogging gangs were defined by the industry most prevalent in that area.

For example, the Gun Quarter was located due north of the town center and was gathered around St. Chad's Roman Catholic Cathedral. Here, the gunmakers initially reigned supreme, but when the Birmingham Small Arms Company set up new factories outside the town in 1861, the housing and fortune of the occupants in the Gun Quarter deteriorated. It was then that this area became renowned for its toughness. Stone-throwing, or slogging, became commonplace, even against those police officers who would dare to intervene. It is also true that not all occupations had only one territory—many, such as pearl-button makers and brass workers, controlled territories in various parts of town.

Cheapside was one of the longer streets in Birmingham, and it had a particularly bad reputation. It was there that the organized slogging gangs originated in the early 1870s. Even the boarding schools that were built between 1870 and 1871 had their own slogging gangs—there was a well-known rivalry between boarding school slogging gangs and church school slogging gangs. In fact, it was these boarding schools that would introduce a new pattern of living to Birmingham residents.

Chapter Three

Youth Gangs

"The civility which money will purchase, is rarely extended to those who have none."

—Charles Dickens

In 1870 and 1871, Birmingham experienced changes that brought about a new pattern of life, particularly for children. Children used to work with their parents from an early age through to their teens, but now that old pattern was interrupted by school, which resulted in the postponement of work until the age of 11 or 12. Still, for many children, the only home they knew was the street, and their education involved learning to survive.

Many of Birmingham's children were street beggars on the verge of criminality. These legions of abandoned children began to organize themselves into youth gangs, which became known for creating all sorts of problems throughout the town. For these children, the gang was an important part of their socialization, and for many, the gang was their only family and source of entertainment. The gang also provided these young people with a way to make money. They engaged in various forms of criminal activity such as shoplifting and pickpocketing, and they were also known for committing various levels of assault. They preyed upon younger children as well as adults, and they often adopted pubs as places for many of their activities, including drinking and gambling.

Beginning in the late 1860s, the newspapers reported on juvenile gang activities, including fights between rival gangs. The first use of the term "slogging gang" occurred in April of 1872 and was in reference to a group of approximately 400 rough youths in Cheapside. Cheapside had a small but significant Irish enclave, and it was these youths that organized themselves into a slogging gang. They smashed windows and forced shopkeepers to shutter their windows against mud, brickbats, and even dead dogs. This became known as the stone riot, and the rioters terrorized the neighborhood until police were finally able to disperse them. After this time, slogging riots and battles became more commonplace in Birmingham.

An economic boom occurred in 1872 as foreign wars boosted gun manufacture and sales. The workers saw an opportunity to bargain for better wages and organized numerous strikes, many of which ended in violent riots. This only excited the activities of the slogging gangs, which became more adventurous in nature. One band even took possession of a polling booth and stopped voting until the police were able to clear them out. Then, as the strike fever that resulted from the economic boom began to die down, it was replaced by slogging fever. This would lead to what could be called the first peak in March of 1873.

On March 30, a Sunday, Birmingham experienced an explosion of slogging that lasted for several hours. There were no less than five riot outbreaks in different parts of town. The violence left the police stretched to the breaking point, and the townspeople were in a state of shock. There had been several violent incidents in the weeks prior to this outbreak, but the cause has never been fully explained or remedied.

One week prior to this incident, there had been a major disturbance after five constables arrived to disperse some boys living in a ruined house in Livery Street. The boys pelted the constables with brickbats. When the officers finally apprehended 14 of the youths, a large crowd began following them, throwing mud and stones. Later, when a police van came to take them to the Moor Street lock-up, a mob of approximately 100 men and women had gathered to continue harassing the police. That evening, about one-half mile from this location, there was another small riot between young men from the Gun Quarter and youths from another district to the southeast.

Still, these incidents were small in comparison to the riot that broke out on March 30th. Around 2 pm, a police sergeant named Parkinson, along with two constables, went to a house in Cheapside to arrest a man, but when they emerged with their prisoner, a large crowd began to form. Soon, the crowd numbered more than 1,000 as it followed the police officers and their prisoner. The crowd then began throwing stones. At approximately the same time, police officers were also attacked by mobs in Newtown Row and Great Queen Street, and in other parts of town, passersby were targeted by groups. By the time the incidents were over, some 15 people had been arrested, and predictably, the press was outraged, noting that there had now been some 11 weeks of violent incidents. The police responded by calling on every citizen to aid them in their efforts to calm the situation.

During the investigation, it emerged that certain streets were being used as meeting places for sloggers. Yet, despite the best efforts of the police, the violence continued. One month after the huge riot on March 30, the police were once again put to the test when a slogging gang of approximately 100 boys began throwing stones and smashing windows on Bagot Street. The residents had to shutter their windows against the violence, but one man was still injured and had to go to the hospital. Soon, the violence spread to various other parts of town as slogging became the fashion in Birmingham. The situation became so bad that the press reported that mob law reigned on Saturday nights and Sundays in parts of town. It was commonplace to see mobs of several hundred gathering for slogging. Whenever sloggers were arrested for their behavior, their friends would begin stoning the police as they dragged their prisoners away. Several police officers were injured by these attacks.

Slogging attacks continued throughout the year of 1873, and they often occurred in the aftermath of a major strike. Three strikes, in particular, affected the violence. The first was the defeat of the farm laborers who wanted a living wage, the second was the strike of the nut and bolt makers who won and received their demands, and the third was a victory for the chain makers in their fight for increased pay. How much these strikes might have influenced the activities of slogging gangs is unknown, but there were major slogging riots following each of these strikes.

As the violence escalated, it was only a matter of time before someone was killed, and the first death occurred in Cheapside in an incident between the Milk Street gang and the Park Street gang. A 15-year-old boy by the name of John Thomas Kirkham died from injuries he received after being stabbed in the neck. He identified his attackers from his hospital bed, where he lay critically ill for four weeks before dying. Though Kirkham denied any involvement in a slogging gang, it was alleged he was the leader of the Milk Street gang. The young boy who stabbed him was sentenced to a month's imprisonment. Later, at age 19, he would be sentenced to four months of hard labor for an unprovoked attack on two men.

After this incident, the slogging violence continued, though it was no longer restricted to Cheapside and Milk Street. In 1874, there was a kind of fighting competition among the slogging gangs. They fought each other until several were injured and the police got involved to end the fighting. At that time, any boy who refused to join a gang was reportedly stoned.

In July, there was another huge riot known as the Bordesley Riot. It started when a witness who had given testimony against an Irish boy for throwing stones at a policeman was spotted by a slogging gang. They followed the witness to his house, where they first stoned the house and later the police who arrived to restore order. The mob was estimated at over 500 strong, but the constables managed to arrest the leaders. By the end of the riot, the size of the crowd was said to be larger than 1,000.

Over time, it became clear that the police were on trial as much as were the sloggers. The problem had no easy solution, however, because part of the problem was the overcrowding of this large industrial city. Additionally, the riots were often alcohol-fueled, and stone-throwing had become an accepted part of Birmingham street culture. For their part, the police were undermanned, and charged with enforcing draconian laws. With no easy solution, the problems continued to grow until there was an outcry for corporal punishment—flogging. A lull in slogging activity calmed the panic that resulted in the outcry for this type of punishment. Instead, it appeared that tougher sentences handed down by magistrates were helping. A royal visit by the prince and princess of Wales went off without a hitch, but by 1875, Birmingham would once again find itself besieged with gang violence. In March of that year, a police constable named William Lines was stabbed in the ear and later died from his wounds. His attacker received the death sentence, and his accomplices received life in penal servitude for their roles in the attack.

Despite the stiffer penalties and the lull in activity, gang violence would see a resurgence. By 1887, gang violence was once more running rampant in the streets of Birmingham. There was a lot of activity in Bordesley where the gang there was often blamed for highway robbery. Belts had become a favorite weapon, and the use of a belt in a crime at that time almost always resulted in a prison sentence. By this time, slogging—like crime—ran in families, and familial affiliations were linked to territories. By 1889, gangs were routinely invading one another's territory, and overcrowding had again become a serious problem, spurring more violence. This set the stage for the rise of the Peaky Blinders.

Chapter Four

Rise of the Peaky Blinders

"A serious assault was committed upon a young man named George Eastwood . . . Several men known as the 'Peaky Blinders' gang, whom Eastwood knew by sight from their living in the same neighborhood as himself, came in."

—*The Birmingham Mail, 1890*

The Peaky Blinders were formed when one of the most violent slogging gangs of young men and boys resisting police crackdowns on crime became more formally organized and started to run the streets of Birmingham. They likely derived their name from the peaked hat all of the members wore. These caps were often referred to as peaky. It's not clear what the term blinders refers to. The popular story is that the gang members would sew razor blades into the peaks of their caps, and then attack someone by headbutting them with their cap. The razor would cut the head of the unfortunate victim and cause blood to pour into their eyes, thereby blinding them—thus, the name Peaky Blinders. Historians note, however, that razor blades, as we now know them, were a new invention and a luxury item at that time. Therefore, it is unlikely these gang members would have had them and sewn them into their caps.

Another suggestion is that the gang members would use their hat to hide their identity, thereby keeping their victims from seeing them. Still another idea is that they often came up behind their victims and pulled the hat down over their victim's eyes so they were blinded to their identity. Finally, one last suggestion is that the term blinders referred to particularly attractive people at that time. Since the gang members dressed elegantly, they were considered blinders.

Whatever the truth about their name, the Peaky Blinders were likely founded in Small Heath—a downtrodden suburb of Birmingham. The first reference to the Peaky Blinders was about a violent gang operating in Bordesley. A street there, Adderley Street, which was close to the border between Bordesley and Small Heath, contained several factories—one for gasworks, one for iron smelting, and one for copper smelting. Because of this, this area was one of the most polluted parts of Birmingham, and it had a bad reputation for gangs. Highway robbery and assault were common crimes in the area, and holiday fights were frequent. One such fight on Easter Monday in 1889 left a man lying in the street unconscious with a compound depressed skull fracture. A policeman told the barrister that the attackers were members of a slogging gang.

Shortly after this, an assault took place in a pub on Adderley Street. A newspaper article in 1890 detailed the assault on George Eastwood, a Small Heath resident. The article mentions that Eastwood recognized his attackers as Peaky Blinders and that they lived in the same neighborhood as he did. Eastwood identified Thomas Mucklow as the leader of the gang, and Mucklow would serve nine months in hard labor for his role in the attack.

Mucklow was also associated with another Adderley Street laborer named John Gavin, who had been imprisoned for three months in 1888 for attacking a policeman. This was the gang that became known as the Peaky Blinders.

Whatever the nature of their founding, the Peaky Blinders would rise to power on the dangerous streets of Birmingham, and they would take control of the area for the next decade. Within five years of their first mention, the term Peaky Blinders would come to refer to gangs in general, but one of the first individuals to be publicly referred to as a Peaky Blinder was a metal roller from the east side of the city named Henry Lightfoot. He was notorious for his convictions for theft and for his association with gangs. He had an extensive criminal record and was considered more than a slogger. This marked a trend of more hardened criminals becoming involved with what used to be the slogging gangs.

Both Small Heath and Bordesley were extremely poor slums, and as the Peaky Blinders began to organize themselves, occupying favorable territory became their first order of business. To do that, they had to fight a rival group known as the Cheapside Sloggers. The Cheapside Sloggers, led by John Adrian, had run the area since 1870 using protection rackets and violence. Soon, the Peaky Blinders were able to take over. With the defeat of the Cheapside Sloggers, the Peaky Blinders were able to establish the territory they controlled, and they became well-known throughout that territory for both their violence and their appearance.

Peaky Blinders were easily recognizable by their manner of dress. Gang members all wore tailored jackets, lapel overcoats, button waistcoats, silk scarves, bell-bottom pants, leather boots, and their signature peaked hats. The *Birmingham Weekly Post* described the specifics of the carefully stylized appearance of the Peaky Blinders and noted the trousers were 22 inches around the bottom and 15 inches around the knee. The scarf they wore, referred to as a silk daff, was twisted twice around their necks and tied at the ends. Once in place, it was referred to as a choker. They often wore bowler hats with the brim fit to the side and the front coming to a point, almost like the sprout of a jug. They accomplished this by wetting the brim and warming it by the fire so they could shape it. They wore this hat on one side of the head so that their hair on the other side, done in a style known as a quiff, could be seen. They also used so-called snakes to clasp the belts rather than buckles, and since these were supposedly less harmful when wielded as a weapon, they used that as a defense in slogging trials. It didn't work well to get their sentences reduced, however.

The Peaky's moll, or girlfriend, also had a distinctive style. She sported a lavish display of pearl buttons, a well-developed fringe that obscured the whole of her forehead to the level of her eyes, and a silk handkerchief covering her throat. The Peaky Blinders were as violent to their molls as they were to other victims, and it frequently led to injury. Still, the molls stuck by their men. One reportedly declared, "No, I shouldn't like him as well if he didn't knock me about a bit." Another Peaky Blinder stabbed his girl in the back when she refused to go with him one night. Her mother later told the court that he frequently beat her daughter with a stick. Another case resulted in the tragic death of 18-year-old Emily Pimm. Her boyfriend kicked her to death while wearing boots with metal tips. Yet another case involved a Peaky Blinder who had split up with his girlfriend after a two-year relationship. She was pregnant with his child, and when he happened to see her later, she spoke to him and he responded by violently kicking her in the abdomen. She suffered a miscarriage as a result.

It is clear that the dapper appearance of the Peaky Blinders was only matched by their violent nature. In fact, violence was a hallmark of the life of a Peaky Blinder. Once established, as the gang began the process of expanding their territory, they committed numerous acts of assault and robbery. They targeted anyone who had something they wanted. It made no difference if they were male or female, young or old, rich or poor.

The Peaky Blinders also began to recruit new members, and they regularly recruited from among the desperate children on the streets of Birmingham. Among their prominent members were David Taylor, who was jailed for carrying a gun at age 13, and Charles Lambourne, 12 years old. They never lacked for willing members. Oftentimes, it wasn't possible to tell how many members were in the gang, because some men would don the appropriate apparel and fight just for the status that being a Peaky Blinder afforded them.

The more notorious members of the gang would include a man named Kevin Mooney, whose real name was Thomas Gilbert. He routinely changed his name, and he was responsible for initiating numerous land grabs for the gang. Another prominent member was a man named Harry Fowles, who became known as Baby-Faced Harry. He was arrested at age 19 for bicycle theft. Other well-known members were Earnest Haynes and Stephen McNickle, both of whom were arrested for bike theft and home invasion. The police described them as "foul-mouthed young men who stalk the streets in drunken groups, insulting and mugging passersby." Such was the reputation of the Peaky Blinder on the streets of Birmingham.

Chapter Five

Mob Rule

"No matter what part of the city one walks, gangs of 'peaky blinders' are to be seen, who ofttimes think nothing of grossly insulting passers by, be it a man, woman or child."

—Anonymous letter sent to the *Birmingham Daily Mail* in 1898.

From 1890 onward, the mobs ruled the streets of Birmingham. In 1890, the death of Arthur Hyde outside of the Canterbury Music Hall resulted in riots that caused the local newspaper to declare that a state of mob law had arisen in the streets. Stabbings and assaults on policemen were at an all-time high, and gangs could be found in the suburbs as well as the inner city. Highway robberies were common and made Birmingham a dangerous place for outsiders. The economic boom that had occurred in the previous 20 years did little to ease tensions, and in fact, the newspaper connected the rise in gang activity to the revival in trade. The situation was so bad that citizens weren't even safe in the middle of the day, and in Birmingham, the gang activity was widespread throughout the city as compared to other cities where it was confined to certain districts.

With the increase in gang activity, the violence no longer only involved young men. Older men—25 to 35 years old—increasingly became involved in gangs, and some of these built fearsome reputations. "Bluey" Byers, for example, had 39 convictions for drunk and disorderly conduct by the time he was 32 years old. Others, like Gunner Pimm, were constantly in and out of prison for fighting. Pimm's wife, just as violent as he was, attacked a detective who tried to arrest her husband. This trend of older gang members marked a new era in gang activity, and the violence took on a more severe nature as a result. The Peaky Blinders were among the worst, and more police were deployed to the areas in which they were most active.

Still, the violence continued spreading. Though Bordesley and Small Heath were the centers for much of the unrest, adjacent areas such as Bordesley Green were becoming ever more dangerous as well. Attacking policemen became increasingly common. One older gang member, 35-year-old John Gilhooley, developed what could only be called a pathological addiction to assaulting constables. As a teen, he had served three sentences for attacking policemen, the longest of which was seven years for breaking one constable's jaw and biting another's hand.

By August of 1893, there were nearly nightly fights waged by as many as 500 gang members near the Gun Quarter, and here again, an older gang member, Michael Surr, took great pleasure in stirring up mob violence whenever the police attempted to make an arrest. The press reported on his 47th court appearance in this same year of 1893. By 1895, Henry Lightfoot was likely the leader of the Peaky Blinders, and the police considered him to be "a 'peaky blinder' of a dangerous type." By age 22, he already had several convictions for burglary and assault.

As the Peaky Blinders expanded their territory, they also began to grow their criminal enterprise. Though some historians argue their activities were focused more on street fighting, robbery, and racketeering rather than organized crime, the Peaky Blinders were increasingly involved in fraud, land grabs, smuggling, hijacking, and illegal bookmaking as well. As their enterprise expanded, they grew bolder, frequently attacking rival gangs and the police. They deliberately targeted police in activities they dubbed "constable baiting."

In 1897, a member of the gang killed Constable George Snipe, and his death would become the *cause célèbre* of 1897. Snipe was on duty in Hockley Hill on July 18, when he became involved in a confrontation involving youth gangs. He arrested a man named Colrain, who resisted violently. As he and another constable moved the man along, a large crowd gathered and began throwing stones and bricks. One stone hit Snipe in the head and knocked him unconscious. He was taken to the hospital where he died four hours later. George Snipe, who was one of the first officers put on the police force Roll of Honour for his sacrifice while serving, died of two skull fractures he received from that blow to the head.

Snipe's funeral would draw over 200 policemen, who lined the streets along the route from the church to the cemetery. A public collection was made to support his widow and baby. The man accused of causing his death was James Franklin, and while Snipe's colleagues were collecting money to support his family, Franklin's friends were going house to house to collect money for his defense. Witnesses came forward to say they had seen someone else do it, and that the culprit had already left Birmingham. The case against Franklin was weakening, and those witnesses who were willing to testify against him were demanding police protection. While Franklin was charged with willful murder, another suspect emerged, a man named "Cloggy" Williams. Williams was said to have actually wielded the brick who killed Snipe, but he had since disappeared. Meanwhile, the trial against Franklin proceeded.

Franklin's trial attracted enormous interest. The key prosecution witness was a woman named Polly Mullins. She claimed to have seen Franklin throw the lethal brick, and she was at Snipe's side when he fell. She denied seeing anyone resembling Williams, nor did she know him. In response to the prosecution's case, the defense called a man named James "Chicken" Jones. He gave the fullest explanation of what had happened that day. He claimed that he was in a tavern with Williams when they went out and saw the policeman with Colrain. He said Williams threw the brick, and then the two of them walked off along Bridge Street together. The next day, he left to visit his sister in Bolton, and Williams insisted on going with him. Williams then disappeared from Bolton after learning that Snipe had died of his injuries.

Jones's sister confirmed this story, and with such strong evidence, Franklin was acquitted to a loud burst of applause from the courtroom gallery. For his part, Cloggy Williams was finally arrested in early 1898 after returning to Birmingham to visit his mother. He was charged with murder and later admitted throwing the brick, though he said he did it because he thought the policeman was a man named Holdsworth. Holdsworth bore a striking physical resemblance to Snipe, and thus, it was a case of mistaken identity that resulted in his death. Williams was convicted of manslaughter and sentenced to life in penal servitude.

Chapter Six

The Law Strikes Back

"In its purest form, an act of retribution provides symmetry. The rendering payment of crimes against the innocent. But a danger on retaliation lies on the furthering cycle of violence. Still, it's a risk that must be met; and the greater offense is to allow the guilty go unpunished."

—Emily Thorne

The death of Constable Snipe would spark uproar among the citizens of Birmingham, who demanded that something be done. On July 26, 1897, there was what was referred to as an indignation meeting at the Smith Street Boarding School. The accusation was made that the magistrates living in more peaceful parts of town were unaware of the habits of the Peaky Blinders and that they didn't understand what the working people had to suffer at their hands. They accused the magistrates of being too hard on the constables who resorted to physical force when confronting the ruffians.

By the end of the meeting, all were in agreement that the only answer to street violence was flogging. People also wanted stiffer penalties for assaults, particularly those on women and the police, and they pointed to evidence that these measures were effective. Charles Henry Street was, at one time, notorious for the activity of Peaky Blinders, especially on Saturday nights, but after the imposition of stricter prison sentences, the shops on the street all had tenants and were doing well.

To understand how lenient the courts were toward these offenders, the statistics showed that in over 150 cases of assault on police in the previous three months before July of 1897, only approximately one-third of the offenders had been imprisoned without the option of a fine. The longest prison sentence handed out had been only four months. There was also the suggestion that compulsory military service might be the answer, particularly since so many of the offenders were young men and boys. Others argued that the public should be armed.

Over the next three years, there were a higher number of convictions and harsher sentences, but the level of gang violence remained high. By 1900, nine officers on the Birmingham police force had been disabled because of assault. One of the officers was then found guilty of unjustified force, and this exacerbated an already inflammatory situation.

Once again, the surrounding suburbs saw various acts of violence with numerous gang clashes and assaults. There was also an increase in assaults involving firearms. Revolvers were easy to acquire and inexpensive—costing as little as a shilling and sixpence (less than one British pound)—and an increasing number of gang members carried them. This led one judge to recommend that children under 15 who carried revolvers should be whipped instead of being sent to prison. By 1900, the possession of a loaded gun at the scene of a crime was, in and of itself, considered incriminating evidence and therefore carried heavy penalties.

Despite the efforts to implement harsher sentences for gang violence, by 1900, the Peaky Blinders still reigned in the city centers. They paraded the streets, committing highway robbery at will and terrorizing shopkeepers. In Bordesley Green, the shopkeepers lived in fear of gang members they were too frightened to prosecute. So feared were the Peaky Blinders that the name had caught on nationwide. Even new scientific discoveries of microbes were described by the notorious term. One Manchester newspaper noted about new discoveries by Pasteur and the Curies that, "You can scarcely walk a yard without meeting a gang of peaky blinder microbes ready to commit assault and battery."

The emergence of so-called hooligans in other parts of the country also drew comparisons to the Peaky Blinders of Birmingham. But change was coming, and it would eventually bring an end to the reign of terror the Peaky Blinders had enjoyed for more than ten years in Birmingham.

Chapter Seven

Life Changes in Birmingham

"[The Peaky Blinders'] actions were mostly restrained to rival gangs and the police. The general public was seldom interfered with unless they interfered."

—F. Atkins, the Birmingham Weekly Post, 1936.

The changing life in Birmingham in the latter part of the nineteenth century and the beginning of the twentieth century had a profound impact on the citizens and on youth gang activity. Birmingham was considered Britain's industrial heartland, and as noted, it became the center for the production of metal-based goods. Part of the reason for this was that there were local reserves of raw materials, including coal and iron ore. Another fact that created this situation was that renowned engineers—such as James Brindley and Thomas Telford—helped develop a complex canal network, which placed Birmingham at the center of the national canal network. That made it easy to transport raw materials to local factories and the finished goods to markets throughout the country.

Another factor that affected the fortunes of this growing city was the arrival of the railways in the mid-nineteenth century. The railways eventually became the primary method for transportation of raw materials as the canal network fell into decline. The growth of industrial factories resulted in a wide range of goods that were produced in Birmingham, and it eventually became known as "the city of a thousand trades." Gun making was one of those trades, and during the Napoleonic Wars, over three million gun barrels were manufactured in Birmingham. Jewelry was another common trade, and a large proportion of the country's fine jewelry was manufactured in the city.

The rapid growth of these industries caused the city's population to soar. By 1901, the population was 522,204, and waves of immigrants swarming the city were part of the reason for the rapid growth. Irish and Italian communities were established, and as discussed, ethnicity played a large role in the activities of the slogging gangs that emerged from the despair created by the overcrowded conditions. The rapid population growth also led to a number of health problems that accompanied poor housing and sanitation. With the passing of the Municipal Charter in 1838, many of these problems began to be addressed, but it wouldn't be until later that Birmingham's civic leaders would be able to take the appropriate steps to improve sanitation and public health.

The catalyst for this transformation was Joseph Chamberlain, who was elected as Birmingham's mayor in 1873. He served in that position for three years before going on to become one of Birmingham's parliamentary members in 1876. As mayor, Chamberlain took steps to improve public services, and he also developed many schemes to improve the town in general. He helped Birmingham weather the Long Depression that began in

1873 and lasted through 1879. It severely affected Europe at this time, but Chamberlain helped Birmingham fare better than most. His efforts led to the transformation of the city. His initiatives led to the municipal control of the city's supply of gas and water as well as the clearance of slum housing in several areas of the city center in 1875. Chamberlain also used public and private money for the construction of libraries, swimming pools, parks, schools, and various other civic buildings.

In 1889, Birmingham was granted city status, and by that time, gas, electricity, water, roads, sewers, lighting, sanitary arrangements, public transportation, and the police force were all under municipal control. Additionally, the city saw the opening of the first municipal hospitals, schools, parks, and even public baths. Many of Birmingham's citizens had a renewed sense of pride in their city. In the first years of the twentieth century, Birmingham physically expanded, allowing for more people to move to the area. Its population reached a peak in 1951 of 1.1 million. Today, it boasts approximately 1 million inhabitants.

Birmingham's Lunar Society meeting made distinctive contributions to education in the city. The Hill family made significant contributions in this area since their progressive methods of school organization, curricula, and teaching had developed a reputation internationally. The groups backing these educational methods helped institute the national elementary education from 1870 onward. In 1900, the University of Birmingham opened its doors, and in the twentieth century, this university led the way in providing racial and gender equality in education. These kinds of progress led to Birmingham being called an "enlightened city of education."

It was in this context that Birmingham's slogging gangs, and eventually the Peaky Blinders, came to prominence. Throughout the ups and downs of Birmingham's fortunes, the Peaky Blinders prevailed. Though the education reforms caused some leaders to declare that the problem of juvenile gangs had been solved, by 1894, it was widely understood that was not the case. The superintendent of the Ashton police force had increased the force by more than 400 constables, and his efforts were cited in 1898 as being responsible for the repression of slogging gangs, and by the time of the Birmingham Fair that year, it seemed as though gang violence was a distant memory.

Extreme nationalism, called jingoism, swept through Birmingham with the outbreak of the Second Boer War in October of 1899, and that seemed to engage most of the youthful energies, particularly when it became evident that victory was at hand in 1900. All seemed well, but when the Liberal MP David Lloyd George came to Birmingham and accused the Chamberlain family of war profiteering, violence once again broke out. A riotous demonstration occurred in which 1 person was killed, 28 civilians were injured, and 97 policemen were hurt. By the summer of that year, the territory of the Peaky Blinders was restricted to the city center. Along Garrison Lane, gang members robbed people and regularly threw bricks at passersby. There were also multiple acts of vandalism.

At this time, football was gaining popularity, even though it was outlawed in the street and on some school playgrounds. Still, as its popularity grew, many youths were drawn to this sport rather than involvement in gangs. By 1900, it seemed that slogging gangs were passing into history. Remnants remained, such as on Garrison Lane, where slogging riots still occurred most evenings in the summer of 1901, but the scale and intensity of the gang wars would only rarely be repeated at this time.

Chapter Eight

Peaky Blinders: The End of an Era

"Even gang members imagine a future that doesn't include gangs."

—Greg Boyle

The end of the nineteenth century would see a number of changes around the world that would result in a decline in gang violence and the eventual demise of the Peaky Blinders. Youth energies were increasingly drawn to the ever more popular sport of football, and the expansion of the suburbs and the establishment of reliable telephone communications restricted gang territory to a few city center locations. With the new century came new terminology describing youthful offenders. Increasingly, the terms "hooligans" and "hooliganism" replaced sloggers and even Peaky Blinders. "Peaky" behavior was increasingly seen as individual rather than collective in nature.

A number of factors likely contributed to the decrease in gang activities. The increase in the severity of the punishments handed out for gang behavior and better police organization played significant roles, but so did better education and provisions for Birmingham's young people.

Additionally, there was a decrease in publicity surrounding gang activities, and that, too, may have played a role in their eventual demise. As well, the rise of other forms of leisure activity—such as football—that were far less risky and more satisfying than being a part of a gang played a role in the demise of the gangs. Physical altercations took on new forms, such as boxing. These factors also altered the behavior of the remaining gangs. Their criminal behavior took on other forms, such as organized intimidation and gambling. Also, during this time, the Edwardian Children's Act was introduced. It created juvenile courts and a growing number of agencies for dealing with troubled youth.

Still, the Peaky Blinders had not entirely disappeared. Though the enlargement of the city had increased the distance between the gang-controlled territories, personal followings would continue to be important, and there were still groups that had significant power to bully and create general mayhem. Additionally, group competition survived as did adolescent peer pressure. These factors would ensure that the gangs would never completely disappear.

In the early 1900s, Birmingham would be engaged in solving other problems. Because of the rapid population growth, water supply had remained a constant problem. In 1891, construction of the Elan aqueduct had been approved, and it would continue until the project's completion in 1904. The focus on improvements into the early 1900s kept Birmingham residents employed and busy. In 1903, the first motor buses would begin to operate in the city, and the New Hudson Bicycle Company would begin producing New Hudson motorcycles. In 1906, the city would see the completion of the St. Andrews Football Stadium. Between 1907 and 1913, a number of new public facilities would open as well as a number of new businesses and educational facilities. Birmingham was growing and becoming more modern.

As for the Peaky Blinders, they had expanded into racecourses, and that had caught the attention of a larger gang, the Birmingham Boys. The Peaky Blinders' activity at the racetracks brought a violent backlash from the Birmingham Boys, and that led to many Peaky Blinder families moving from Birmingham's city center. Most dispersed into the countryside around the city. When that happened, the Sabini gang moved in and challenged the Birmingham Boys, and with their defeat, the Sabini gang solidified their political control over central England well into the 1930s.

Chapter Nine

The World Moves On: World War I

"Only the dead have seen the end of war."

—George Santayana

There were a number of factors that led to the start of what was known as "the war to end all wars." One factor was the alliances that many countries had made with their neighbors. Russia was allied with Serbia, Germany with Austria-Hungary, France with Russia, Britain and France with Belgium, and Japan with Britain. When Austria-Hungary declared war on Serbia, it triggered a number of events that eventually pulled these allies into a worldwide conflict. First, Russia entered the war to defend Serbia, then Germany was drawn in to support Austria-Hungary and declared war on Russia. That ensured that France was drawn in as well in defense of Russia. Germany attacked France by marching through Belgium, and that pulled Britain into the war. That brought Japan in, and later, Italy and the United States.

Another factor that affected the start of the war was that an arms race had begun with numerous countries increasing the number of their warships and the size of their armies. That increased the militarism that helped encourage countries to become involved in the war. Additionally, imperialism would lead to competing claims in Africa and parts of Asia. That increased tensions between European countries and led to a desire for larger empires. It also led to the desire of certain groups to be independent, particularly the Slavic peoples of Bosnia and Herzegovina, who no longer wanted to be part of Austria-Hungary. Instead, they wanted to be part of Serbia. That, specifically, led to a nationalistic and ethnic revolt that led directly to the assassination of Archduke Franz Ferdinand, which was the proximate cause of the war.

In June of 1914, a Serbian nationalist terrorist group known as the Black Hand sent various groups to assassinate Archduke Ferdinand of Austria-Hungary. The first attempt failed, but later in the day, a Serbian nationalist named Gavrilo Princip was successful in shooting and killing the archduke and his wife as they were driving through Sarajevo, Bosnia, which was at that time part of Austria-Hungary. That act started World War I.

The effect of the war on Birmingham was devastating. More than 150,000 men from the city, which was more than half of the male population at that time, served in the war, and 13,000 were killed. Another 35,000 were wounded. Despite the terrible human cost, Birmingham was of strategic importance to the war effort, because it was a center of industrial production, which became focused on the production of war goods at the start of the war. At the end of the war, Britain's Prime Minister David Lloyd George even recognized the significance of the city to the allied victory.

Many Peaky Blinder gang members were also veterans of the First World War. Henry Lightfoot, for example, joined the army three times in his life. In World War I, he participated in the Battle of the Somme in 1916. Another member of the gang, Henry Fowler, was buried alive in the trenches, and such was his trauma, that he couldn't speak or see for a while following the war. Thus, though the Peaky Blinder gang activities had all but disappeared, the Peaky Blinders were still fighting.

Chapter Ten

The Enduring Legacy of the Peaky Blinders

"I'm not a traitor to my class. I am just an extreme example of what a working man can achieve."

—Thomas Shelby in BBC's *Peaky Blinders*

Nearly 40 years after the demise of the Peaky Blinders, their memory was stirred by letters published in the "Notes and Queries" column of the *Birmingham Weekly Post*. One correspondent wrote about how he had been a witness to many of the Peaky Blinders' bad acts. Another reader replied, insisting that the Peaky Blinder was simply an ordinary working man, found at work during the day, just "doing his bit at the lathe or vice or perhaps as a polisher or in the casting shop." F. Atkins, another correspondent, also argued that many readers had a misconception of Peaky Blinders. Their actions, he said, were restricted to rival gangs and the police, and they rarely attacked the general public. He also gave a detailed description of the Peaky Blinders' fashion sense, including their hat. Though they no longer stalked the city streets, their fashion sense, and their violence, made a firm impression on the city's collective memory.

In 2013, their memory was again recalled in the BBC television series *Peaky Blinders*. The story follows the crimes of the Peaky Blinders, but it takes artistic license in the setting. It takes place in post-World War I Birmingham and portrays the fictional Shelby family as the leaders of the gang. Despite its inaccuracies, the show is extremely popular. Another way in which the gang has been memorialized is through the song "Cheapside Sloggers" recorded in 2019 by the Danish metal band Volbeat. The song refers specifically to the Peaky Blinders.

Though the Peaky Blinders are long gone, the gang continues to influence the history of Birmingham. The legend of the well-dressed bandits captured the imagination of an entire nation, and their legacy endures in modern popular culture.

Conclusion

The Peaky Blinders rose to power in the overcrowded and unsanitary conditions of late Victorian Birmingham. The sad reality for children in this polluted, industrial city was that life required them to be street savvy by a very young age. Many were homeless beggars whose only choice was to band together and be prepared to fight at a moment's notice. Their lives were filled with violence, and it's not surprising that many grew into hardened criminals.

As the slogging gangs became widespread throughout Birmingham, a new type of gang arose. This gang was comprised of stylishly dressed members, whose violent nature was matched only by their dapper appearance. They were also called by a new term: Peaky Blinders.

Though they ruled the streets of Birmingham for only a little more than a decade, they built a fearsome reputation. Their riots terrorized the residents of their territory, and no man, woman, or child could safely walk the streets they ruled. Even their own molls were not safe from their violent propensities. The Peaky Blinders left such a mark on the history of Birmingham that even after more than 150 years, they are memorialized in popular culture through song and film.

Printed in Great Britain
by Amazon

30891211R00030